BODY LANGUAGE 10

A MIDSUMMER NIGHT'S PRESS

New York

Main cover photo © 2010 by Nir Arieli *www.nirarieli.com*

A Midsummer Night's Press
16 West 36th Street
2nd Floor
New York, NY 10018
amidsummernightspress@gmail.com
www.amidsummernightspress.com

Designed by Aresográfico *www.diegoareso.com*

First edition, March 2013.

ISBN-13: 978-1-938334-03-0
ISBN-10: 1938334035

Printed in Spain.

CONTENTS

I.

II.

I.

———

ALAN: When I said that I loved you before, you didn't answer me.
ARNOLD: I didn't realize it was a question.
—Harvey Fierstein, *Torch Song Trilogy*

AUBADE

I wish you hadn't spent the night.
At last, the sun is up: please go.
My lover would provoke a fight

if he found you here, despite
our "open relationship." O,
I wish you hadn't spent the night!

I only meant to be polite
to let you stay when sex was through–
I didn't want to risk a fight

when we had just had such delight
from one another's bodies so
I let you spend the night.

But now I think it wasn't right
to give you what was just false hope:
I have a man I love. Don't fight

what is. I'm glad I did invite
you home. We had fun, although
I wish you hadn't spent the night,
my love. Please go now, without a fight.

PALIMPSEST

Can you feel, as your fingers dance across
my back, the marks of all the men
who've touched me before you–
their fingers clawing stripes across my flesh
as we made love, or kneading deep,
as you do, massaging away tension, stress?
I feel that even their lightest caresses
have scarred me permanently, branding me
as surely as the kiss of leather straps and whips.

Is it some sleight of hand trick you do
that makes my body feel fresh and pure?
What is this legerdemain that, although your hands
have traveled this stretch of flesh so many
times before, this path stretching from shoulder
down along the spine to the ass, that makes it seem
new each time, that this is unexplored territory?

Surely your fingers must feel the imprints
of all those earlier passions, as they now awaken
such strong feelings in me again. I open my
mouth to tell you, as I lie before you, naked and
pliable, but your fingers press deep
into muscle–and I lose all will.

THE FROG PRINCE

Lying naked atop the sheets in the summer heat
his lumpy genitals press against his crotch
like a frog crouched
in the thick reeds of his dark pubic hair.

"Kiss me," they whisper,
"and I shall grow into a prince."

ON MEN'S INSECURITIES

What hangs between men's thighs
Has long confirmed their worth.
Men are measured by their size

And, without fail, they'll agonize,
Discontented with birth,
On what hangs between their thighs.

To compensate, each tries
To inflate his pecs' girth,
For men are measured by their size.

Still, it comes as no surprise,
When one's climbed into your berth,
What hangs between his thighs

Swells before your eyes,
Which betray gentle mirth.
Men are measured by their size

And now, when he dies
Le petit mort, no dearth
Hangs between his thighs
And you are measured by his sighs.

TRUST IN BOOKS
for Achy Obejas

I make a list of books to recommend,
visiting an author who's quite well-read;
but for new genres, she trusts the taste of friends.

"Try this," her girlfriend offers, "you can send
it back when you're done." I'm doubtful. Instead,
she makes a list of books she recommends.

I buy extra copies, rather than lend
my own, uncertain they'll ever be read
or returned—even though I trust my friends.

The author and I discuss literary trends.
She says she'll consider what I've said,
and makes her own list, books she recommends.

The books I'd bought her last trip? Still unopened,
low on the stacks of books beside their bed.
So much for trusting the taste of her friends.

Back home, I am prepared to spend
both time and money, but not to be misled.
I read the lists of books they recommend;
Whose taste should I trust, hers or her girlfriend's?

RECIPE FOR LOVE

I can never cook from a book:
all exact and impersonal measurements.
I need someone to show me,
step by step, how it's done.

I'm a lazy cook; I didn't begin
to experiment, to explore, until I was no longer cooking
only for myself.

Let's add a pinch
of this, we'll cook by taste, trying every while
what we're preparing. We'll feed
one another. If something's missing
we'll improvise.

Everything I know about cooking I learned from a friend
who told me: the secret to cooking is to never let
the food smell your fear.

It's also all I know about love.

Let's go into the kitchen
and I'll show you.

CALL BOY

Someone there is that doesn't love a call
    boy's line of work, who notified your folks,
that they might put an end to this career
    you've chosen for yourself: escort/masseur.

Your heart accelerates its steady beat
    when you recognize the flashing number
your beeper's display reveals: *How had they*
    found out? No matter. You must call them back.

You doubt they'll understand, but you are not
    ashamed of what you do. Wary, of course,
in who you tell, for prejudice informs
    many a reaction–but not wary

enough, it seems. Someone opposes this
    oldest of professions. To be desired
is what we all desire, though few admit,
    to others or themselves, how strongly they

possess this feeling–or rather, how this
    yearning possesses them. Your parents fear
for you, that you'll catch AIDS or wind up dead
    in some back alleyway. But sex for sale

these days is almost safer than any
        relationship, where trust might be misplaced
and rash decisions made in the heat of
        passion. "Go ahead and fuck me without

a condom, but just this once." In hustling
        there's a boundary, well defined, of what's
to come—and often, who. No compromise
        is made for love or pity, though someone's

always trying to toe the line. That's fine;
        it merely helps define all the limits.
Good fences make good neighbors, after all;
        it's what these transactions are all about:

distance, disinvolvement, discovery
        of barriers: latex and emotion,
things which keep men wanting more, and coming
        back. Even you. You lift the phone and call.

USING THE POET'S BATHROOM
for Richard Howard

The Greeks were only half correct
that a woman might turn men's flesh hard as stone;
    yours, perhaps, would not grow erect

at the sight of her, but of her own she has
        complete control. Looking inward,
so like mirrors' truths, Maude, too, turned stone: topaz

    gems that floated in her bladder.
You tell this tale to explain why, like a male
        dog, she lifts one leg to splatter

the black plastic bags of garbage with her scent,
        a splendid anecdote about
your discovery that she was a latent

    hermaphrodite. But there is more
at stake than regaling friends on midnight walks
        with Maude, who had waited hours

for your return without an accident. Such
        is the blind devotion of dogs,
that artless strength of will to endure so much

time alone, sustained only by
the idea of your commitment to them. Maude
   held tight to her purpose. The gay

man's best friend, it was not in imitative
   flattery she tried to grow a
penis, but because she recognized your love

   of sameness over difference.
A threshold she could not fully cross, her attempts
   at genital enlargements

contradicted your earlier lines: *a choice*
   that always, when there is a door,
even a French one, must be made. Sacrifice

   her identity, though she tried,
Maude was left whining about sex and her
   crepuscular gender, outside

your bathroom door. In that earlier poem,
   Max, too, whined; for both dogs *the word*
toilet clearly suggests the twilight, some

   subliminal ending. They were
restricted to those parlors overflowing
   with your public life, books and art:

needlepoint pugs on pillows, porcelain pugs,
     pugs in every medium, all gifts.
Pigs, too, for they had monopolized your thoughts

     before your vowels lengthened. On
an island all of vowels, Odysseus
     had come to know and to love swine.

Returned to Ithaca, his sole *memento*
     amori was a piggy bank–
two copulating corpulent pigs into

     whose empty bellies he dropped coins
for his son's wedding. Only his faithful dog,
     after sniffing at the man's loins,

had recognized him. Though too short to reach
     men's crotches, Maude could smell where your
true affections lay. In your bathroom, where flesh

     is exposed from its civilized
garb, ostensibly free from all onlookers
     except that Narcissean gaze,

there is no room for animals. Photographs
     of men cover every surface
(the ceiling even!) as if this were a hive,

each man locked into his own frame
like a cell of memory's honey, and when
　　　the shower fills the room with steam

these boys, unlike bees, do not flee. Mentors, friends,
　　　lovers, the men who have shaped your life,
it was yet too soon to know if I would stand

　　　among their ranks. I stood before
their ancient glittering eyes and unzipped my
　　　pants. I could not hope to compare.

II.

———

"Trust is always a risk—but love is like
god. If you don't have faith in it,
trust in it, it isn't real."

"You don't believe in god," Jonathan said.

"No. But I do believe in love."

—Michelle Sagara West,
"The Vision of Men"

METONYMY

I don't recall the exact phase,
but I remember what book it's from.

I search the entire house but
don't find it. And suddenly I recall

that when we divided our lives,
our books, I let you take it. There is

no gap on the shelves:
other books have filled its space.

Other men have filled your space
in my bed. But the absence of that book

we once shared, that we both
read that summer we met,

opens anew that emptiness inside—
even now, so many years later.

THE PARTY'S OVER

All the guests have already left–
my roommate, too–off partying somewhere.
I'm alone among the full ashtrays and empty
glasses, the remains of a successful birthday
celebration. One by one, I undo the knots
on the balloons, bring them to my lips, and inhale
your breath. I could have gone out, too,
but I don't have the courage to see you hook up with
some other guy, to see those lips (which so recently
inflated these rubber globes, when you helped
us prepare for your friend's party) finding
other lips in some dark corner of a bar. I wanted
to kiss you from the moment you walked through the
                    door,
but you didn't pay me any attention beyond a basic
courtesy. So I chose to remain here, alone and stealing
these kisses of yours from the post-party debris.

AIDS LIMERICK I:
DENYING THE END

These hospital visits portend
that death very soon will attend
     this friend with bold face
     and bear-hug embrace
who begs that I please just pretend.

MIXED SIGNALS

When we meet, at last, you're on your way out
of town. A suitcase beside you, we flirt,
I think, over coffee, but still I doubt

whether this is really a date or not.
Just in case, I carefully chose this shirt.
When we met online, you were in the out-

skirts of Madrid with friends. Even then, I thought
something was off, your typed replies seemed curt.
There's barely time for coffee, so I doubt

if more can come of this. We talk about
our pasts: work, lovers, the usual dirt.
You tell me that, at last, you're moving out

to Sitges, with your dog, a brand-new flat
that's not furnished with memories of hurt,
a chance to start over. But still you doubt.

Meeting you was nice. But our time runs out.
You need to catch your train to the airport.
Will we meet again? Can we work this out?
I'll think it over. But still I doubt.

MUCH ADIEU ABOUT NOTHING

A boy to my left
watched me with questioning blue eyes
    all the while you read.
I ignored that one chance at sex

    tonight; when the lights
came on, I stood and queued to say
goodbye. I passed him, did not say
    anything. He left.

    I stared at the lights
until spots danced before my eyes.
    It was not for sex
I had come here, but to hear you read.

    No, I could have read
your words at home. I came to say,
    "I want to have sex
with you, mentor." Now I am left

    naked before your eyes,
my soul bared beneath these hot lights.
Can't you see me, with the spotlights'
    glare? Then you must read

here what your dark eyes
missed, what I did not, that night, say
     aloud, and thus left
alone, my thoughts, of course, on sex.

     Your poems take sex
for granted; no pleasure or delight
     of the flesh is left
untouched by your pen. When you read,

     anything you say
sounds sexual because your eyes
sparkle. I've tried to catch those eyes
     but, between us, sex

     won't come up. I say
goodnight. You give me a kiss, light,
     on my cheek. I'll read
your poems again, after I've left

     you beneath those lights
where you read; my eyes, your sex, and
     nothing left to say.

UNCOUPLETS

I wrote so many letters to him,
which went unanswered.

I no longer write to him,
but about him.

The poem answers me
with its overwhelming silence.

SKATING BEAUTY

Like the uninvited
thirteenth fairy at the christening,
I am standing just outside
the plaza where they're skating

and I want to curse them
for my not being a part
of such easy youthful
masculine fellowship.

Forget the prick of a finger
on a spinning wheel's needle,
let them crush their hands
beneath the spinning wheels

of their skateboards!
But I want more than just
belonging; it is you I crave:
a beauty that could exist

only in fairy tale,
where magic or alchemy
transforms a catalogue of parts—
eyes, lips, lithe torso that twists

just so at the waist—into something
wondrous and unique, delicate and fierce,
hovering on that threshold
between boyhood and manhood.

Almost shy when on the ground,
unaware of your own desirability,
your board, tucked under your arm
like a shield, blocks the view of your

naked torso as you constantly shift
position, less nervousness than
restless excess of energy.
Then you mount your board.

Everything changes: you are
a modern-day centaur, board and boy
a single being whose grace
and almost preternatural calm

draws the attention of every eye.
Suddenly you launch into the air
legs bent at the knees. You soar,
your board flying up beneath you

and time stops

for a hundred years

with you suspended in this moment

and only a kiss from me
could make it start again.

WINTER DAY

> "...a basket of wine and cake
> to take to her grandmother
> because she was ill.
> Wine and cake?
> Where's the aspirin? The penicillin?"
> —Anne Sexton, *"Little Red Riding Hood"*

Looking for you among these rows of curtained beds
she feel she's lost in some wood, not a hospital ward.
A nurse stops her, asks where she is going,
then directs her to this room. But this is not your face
she see on the pillow, so pale now, a fuzz of hair
all that's left after chemotherapy. Your eyes
look huge behind coke-bottle glasses. "Come closer,"
you whisper. "I've got CMV in that eye."
She's brought you a basket of your favorite foods.
Your appetite is gone these days, but let her believe
it's only because of the hospital fare.
She needs someone to blame for what's happened to you.
If she closes her eyes, your lovers (at least, the ones she'd
        met)
parade before her eyes; which of them deserves reproach?
Which of them is still alive? Do you even know?
She starts to ask you about Marvin, who shaved his legs
        and chest

and wore women's clothes she could only dream of ever
fitting into.

You shiver beneath the thin hospital sheets and her
condemnations

dissolve, unuttered. She looks for blankets. She can't find any,
so she takes off her coat and tucks it around you for warmth.
The red hood sits upon your belly as if you were pregnant,
and she laugh. "That's how it would have been," she says,
meaning, of course, if you and she had married like you
always said you would,

back when you were best friends in college and she still
sometimes thought

a girl like her stood a chance with a boy like you.
The nurse comes in to give you a shot and sends her out.
Downstairs, through a window, she sees snow has begun
to fall.

She's left her coat up in your room, but doesn't go back for it.
You need it more than she. It seems the least she can do.

AIDS LIMERICK II:
LIGHTS OUT

My life has become a motif
of daily compassion and grief,
    of watching the ends
    of lovers and friends
whose candles have been far too brief.

LONG DISTANCE
LOVE POEM
for Marc

He cannot see me, but the boy knows
I am writing about him.
If he is asleep, he rolls over without waking,
as if to fold himself into the curve of my body
until we are like two stacked bowls
filled with each other.
As far as the poem is concerned
this is our sole sustenance,
and if we remember brunching
it was only for the pleasure
of feeding one another.

It is six hours later where he is.
When I miss him, I try to imagine how his life
might be, off-kilter from my own.
If it were the morning, he would be at work–
but I write no poems in the morning.
He is probably asleep now and he is
probably alone.

When the poem ends
he will clutch at the blankets,
pull them around himself

because he feels cold.

I will not stop writing.

DELETING NAMES
(A DECAYING SESTINA)

for Paula

Scrolling through the at-the-limit list of names,
I'm caught unaware: my phone displays a friend
I'll never be able to call again.
Now that all that's left of her are memories
I can't delete her entry, it seems too final,
as if it would erase our entire past together.

Phones are democratic: jumbled together
are lovers and colleagues, name after name
in alphabetical order. It was she who finally
convinced me to get a phone; that day my friend
and I went to buy it is still a vivid memory:

this guy stopped me on the street, total memory
lapse although I knew we'd spent a night together
not long before; both he and my friend
expect an introduction, but I've forgotten his name.

I've now forgotten so many boys; only their names
remain, stored in my phone's memory.
Those I can delete, but not my friend's.

It's as if all that remains of our friendship is this metonymy of her name

on a SIM-card full of memories and names.

ACKNOWLEDGMENTS

Grateful acknowledgment is given to the editors of the following publications in which some of these poems appeared previously, sometimes in earlier versions.

PERIODICALS

Assaracus: "Deleting Names," "Metonymy", "Mixed Signals," "Uncouplets"
Aut (Italy): "The Frog Prince," "Long Distance Love Poem," "Palimpsest"
    (Italian translation by Pierpaolo Perrucci and Alessandro Braghin)
Bay Windows: "Much Adieu About Nothing," "Using the Poet's Bathroom"
Collective Fallout: "Skating Beauty"
Experimental Forest: "Call Boy," "Long Distance Love Poem"
Eye to the Telescope: "Skating Beauty"
First Hand: "The Frog Prince"
Gay and Lesbian Review Worldwide: "Aubade," "Trust in Books"
Gay Scotland: "The Frog Prince"
The Phoenix Review: "The Frog Prince"
Risk (Moscow): "The Frog Prince," "Palimpsest"
    (Russian translations by Dmitry Kuzmin)
Slow Trains: "Long Distance Love Poem"
Van Gogh's Ear: "Using the Poet's Bathroom"

ANTHOLOGIES

120 Pages of Sodom, edited by Iryna Shuvalova, Albina Pozdnyakova and
    Oles Barlig (Kiev, Ukraine: Krytyka): "The Frog Prince," "Metonymy,"
    "Recipe for Love" (Ukranian translations by Olga Lyubarska-Furman)
The Badboy Book of Erotic Poetry, edited by David Laurents (New York:
    Badboy Books): "The Frog Prince," "On Men's Insecurities"
Blanco nuclear. Antología de poesía gay y lésbica última, edited
    by Luis Daniel Pino (Madrid: Sial): "Metonymy," "The Party's Over,"
    "Recipe for Love" (in the original Spanish)
Coming Up: The World's Best Erotic Writing, edited by Michael Perkins,
    New York: Masquerade Books): "The Frog Prince," "On Men's Insecurities"
Ells s'estimen. Poemes d'amor entre homes, edited by Lawrence Schimel
    (Barcelona: Llibres de L'Index): "Long Distance Love Poem," "Palimpsest"
    (Catalan translations by Víctor Planchat)
Erotic Fantasy 2, edited by Justus Roux (Erotictales Publications): "Palimpsest"
From Porn to Poetry 2, edited by Susannah Indigo and Brian Peters (Englewood,
    Colorado: Samba Mountain Press): "Long Distance Love Poem"
Gay Love Poetry, edited by Neil Powell (London: Robinson Books & New York:
    Carroll & Graff): "Palimpsest," "Using the Poets Bathroom"

El libro del voyeur, edited and illustrated by Pablo Gallo (La Coruña, Spain: Ediciones del Viento): "The Frog Prince" (in the author's own Spanish translation)

Mein Heimliches Auge XIX, edited by Claudia Gehrke (Tubingen, Germany: konkursbuch Verlag): "The Frog Prince" (in the author's own German translation)

Mein Schwules Auge VII, edited by Axel Schock (Tubingen, Germany: konkursbuch Verlag): "The Party's Over" (in the author's own English translation)

Men in the 90's, edited by Kerrie Pateman (Peterborough, Scotland: Poetry Now): "On Men's Insecurities"

Moral bi spet priti: sodobna europska gyevska poezija, edited by Brane Mozetic (Ljubljana, Slovenia: Lambda Skuc): "Metonymy" (Slovenian translation by Gasper Malej and Urban Belina), "Recipe for Love" (Slovenian translation by Gasper Malej)

Mythic 2, edited by Mike Allen (Mythic Delirium Books): "Winter Day"

Onzé. XI Festival del poesia de la mediterrània (Palma de Mallorca: Fundació Casa Museu Llorenç Villalonga, Pare Ginard i Blai Bonet): "Aubade," "The Frog Prince," "Much Adieu About Not hing," "Using the Poet's Bathroom" (in English and in Catalan translation by Caterina Calafat)

Of Princes and Beauties: Erotic Fairy Tales, edited by Cecilia Tan (Cambridge Circlet Press): "The Frog Prince"

Queer Dog: Homo/Pup/Poems, edited by Gerry Gomez Pearlberg (San Francisco: Cleis Press): "Using the Poet's Bathroom"

Sextinas. Pasado y presente de una forma poética, edited by Chús Arellano, Jesús Munárriz and Sofía Rhei (Madrid: Hiperion): "Deleting Names" (in both English and Spanish by the author)

Size Counts: A Celebration of the Erection, edited by Inna Zabrodskaya (UK: Diverse Publications): "On Men's Insecurities"

Touched by Eros, edited by George Held (New York: Live Poets Society): "The Frog Prince"

Velvet Heat, edited by Emilie Paris and Scott McMorrow (San Francisco: Pretty Things Press): "The Frog Prince"

Хорошо быть живым, poems and translations by Dmitry Kuzmin (Moscow: Новое литературное обозрение): "The Frog Prince," "Palimpsest" (Russian translations by Dmitry Kuzmin)

"Metonymy," "The Party's Over," and "Recipe for Love" were originally written in Spanish and first appeared in the author's Spanish-language collection *Desayuno en la cama* (Madrid: Desatada/Egales). Translations of "The Frog Prince" and "Palimpsest" into Spanish by the author also appeared in that collection.

LAWRENCE SCHIMEL (New York, 1971) writes in both Spanish and English and has published over 100 books as author or anthologist in many different genres, including one collection of poems written in Spanish, *Desayuno en la cama* (Egales), as well as a chapbook in English, *Fairy Tales for Writers* (A Midsummer Night's Press).

His poems have appeared in diverse periodicals, ranging from *The Christian Science Monitor* to *Physics Today* to *Gay Scotland,* and have been widely anthologized, including in *Gay Love Poetry*, Neil Gaiman's *The Sandman: The Book of Dreams*, *Chicken Soup for the Horse-Lover's Soul 2,* and *The Random House Treasury of Light Verse.*

He has won the Lambda Literary Award (twice), the Spectrum Award, the Independent Publisher Book Award, and the Rhysling Award for poetry, and his picture books have been selected for lists of outstanding titles by the International Board of Books for Youth and by the International Youth Library in Munich, Germany.

His writings have been translated into Basque, Catalan, Croatian, Czech, Dutch, English, Esperanto, Finnish, French, Galician, German, Greek, Hungarian, Icelandic, Indonesian, Italian, Japanese, Korean, Maltese, Polish, Portuguese, Romanian, Russian, Serbian, Slovak, Slovene, Spanish, Turkish, and Ukrainian.

In addition to his own writing, Schimel is a translator from Spanish into English. He has translated poems by Vicente Molina Foix, Luis Antonio de Villena, Jordi Doce, Sofía Rhei, Jesús Encinar, Care Santos, and others for magazines and anthologies including *Agenda, Assaracus, Chroma, Knockout, Mary Quarterly, Pank,* and the *Windy City Times,* among other venues.

A MIDSUMMER NIGHT'S PRESS was founded by Lawrence Schimel in New Haven, CT in 1991. Using a letterpress, it published broadsides of poems by Nancy Willard, Joe Haldeman, and Jane Yolen, among others, in signed, limited editions of 126 copies, numbered 1-100 and lettered A-Z. One of the broadsides —"Will" by Jane Yolen—won a Rhysling Award. In 1993, the publisher moved to New York and the press went on hiatus until 2007, when it began publishing perfect-bound, commercially-printed books, primarily under two imprints:

FABULA RASA: devoted to works inspired by mythology, folklore, and fairy tales. Titles from this imprint include *Fairy Tales for Writers* by Lawrence Schimel, *Fortune's Lover: A Book of Tarot Poems* by Rachel Pollack, *Fairy Tales in Electri-city* by Francesca Lia Block, *The Last Selchie Child* by Jane Yolen, and *What If What's Imagined Were All True* by Roz Kaveney.

BODY LANGUAGE: devoted to texts exploring questions of gender and sexual identity. Titles from this imprint include *This is What Happened in Our Other Life* by Achy Obejas; *Banalities* by Brane Mozetic, translated from the Slovene by Elizabeta Zargi with Timothy Liu; *Handmade Love* by Julie R. Enszer; Mute by Raymond Luczak; *Milk and Honey: A Celebration of Jewish Lesbian Poetry* edited by Julie R. Enszer; *Dialectic of the Flesh* by Roz Kaveney; and *Fortune Light* by David Bergman.